People in My Community/La gente de mi comunidad

Dentist/El dentista

Jacqueline Laks Gorman
photographs by/fotografías de Gregg Andersen

Reading consultant/Consultora de lectura: Susan Nations, M.Ed., author/literacy coach/consultant

Please visit our web site at: www.earlyliteracy.cc
For a free color catalog describing Weekly Reader® Early Learning Library's
list of high-quality books, call 1-877-445-5824 (USA) or 1-800-387-3178 (Canada).
Weekly Reader® Early Learning Library's fax: (414) 336-0164.

Library of Congress Cataloging-in-Publication Data

Gorman, Jacqueline Laks, 1955-
   [Dentist. Spanish & English]
   Dentist = El dentista / by Jacqueline Laks Gorman.
      p. cm. — (People in my community = La gente de mi comunidad)
   Summary: Photographs and simple text introduce the work done by
a dentist.
   Includes bibliographical references and index.
   ISBN 0-8368-3307-4 (lib. bdg.)
   ISBN 0-8368-3341-4 (softcover)
   1. Dentistry—Juvenile literature. 2. Children—Preparation for dental
care—Juvenile literature. [1. Dentists. 2. Occupations. 3. Spanish
language materials—Bilingual.] I. Title: Dentista. II. Title.
RK63.G6718   2002
617.6—dc21   2002066372

This edition first published in 2002 by
Weekly Reader® Early Learning Library
330 West Olive Street, Suite 100
Milwaukee, WI 53212 USA

Copyright © 2002 by Weekly Reader® Early Learning Library

Art direction and page layout: Tammy Gruenewald
Photographer: Gregg Andersen
Editorial assistant: Diane Laska-Swanke
Production: Susan Ashley
Translators: Tatiana Acosta and Guillermo Gutiérrez

Printed in the United States of America

1 2 3 4 5 6 7 8 9 06 05 04 03 02

Note to Educators and Parents

Reading is such an exciting adventure for young children! They are beginning to integrate their oral language skills with written language. To encourage children along the path to early literacy, books must be colorful, engaging, and interesting; they should invite the young reader to explore both the print and the pictures.

People in My Community is a new series designed to help children read about the world around them. In each book young readers will learn interesting facts about some familiar community helpers.

Each book is specially designed to support the young reader in the reading process. The familiar topics are appealing to young children and invite them to read — and re-read — again and again. The full-color photographs and enhanced text further support the student during the reading process.

In addition to serving as wonderful picture books in schools, libraries, homes, and other places where children learn to love reading, these books are specifically intended to be read within an instructional guided reading group. This small group setting allows beginning readers to work with a fluent adult model as they make meaning from the text. After children develop fluency with the text and content, the book can be read independently. Children and adults alike will find these books supportive, engaging, and fun!

Una nota a los educadores y a los padres

¡La lectura es una emocionante aventura para los niños! En esta etapa están comenzando a integrar su manejo del lenguaje oral con el lenguaje escrito. Para fomentar la lectura desde una temprana edad, los libros deben ser vistosos, atractivos e interesantes; deben invitar al joven lector a explorar tanto el texto como las ilustraciones.

La gente de mi comunidad es una nueva serie pensada para ayudar a los niños a conocer el mundo que los rodea. En cada libro, los jóvenes lectores conocerán datos interesantes sobre el trabajo de distintas personas de la comunidad.

Cada libro ha sido especialmente diseñado para facilitar el proceso de lectura. La familiaridad con los temas tratados atrae la atención de los niños y los invita a leer — y releer — una y otra vez. Las fotografías a todo color y el tipo de letra facilitan aún más al estudiante el proceso de lectura.

Además de servir como fantásticos libros ilustrados en la escuela, la biblioteca, el hogar y otros lugares donde los niños aprenden a amar la lectura, estos libros han sido concebidos específicamente para ser leídos en grupos de instrucción guiada. Este contexto de grupos pequeños permite que los niños que se inician en la lectura trabajen con un adulto cuya fluidez les sirve de modelo para comprender el texto. Una vez que se han familiarizado con el texto y el contenido, los niños pueden leer los libros por su cuenta. ¡Tanto niños como adultos encontrarán que estos libros son útiles, entretenidos y divertidos!

— Susan Nations, M.Ed., author, literacy coach,
and consultant in literacy development

The dentist has an important job. The dentist takes care of people.

- - - - - - -

El trabajo del dentista es muy importante. El dentista cuida de la gente.

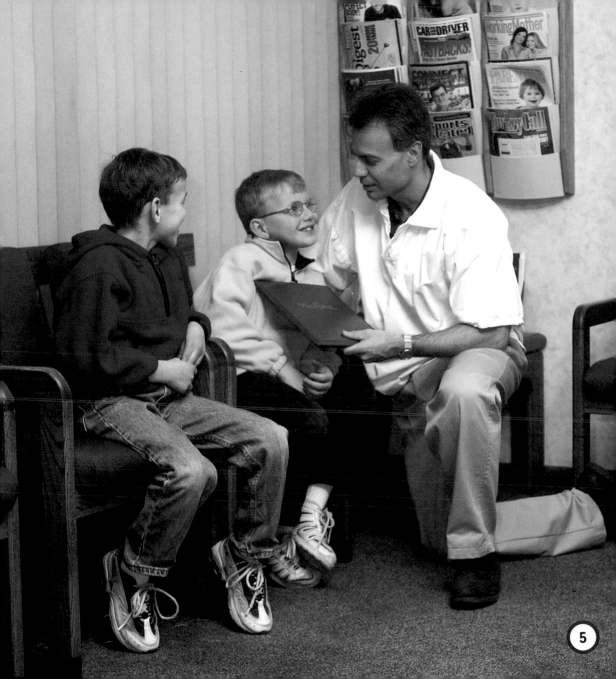

The dentist takes care of your mouth. The dentist takes care of your teeth.

— — — — — — — —

El dentista te cuida la boca. El dentista te cuida la dentadura.

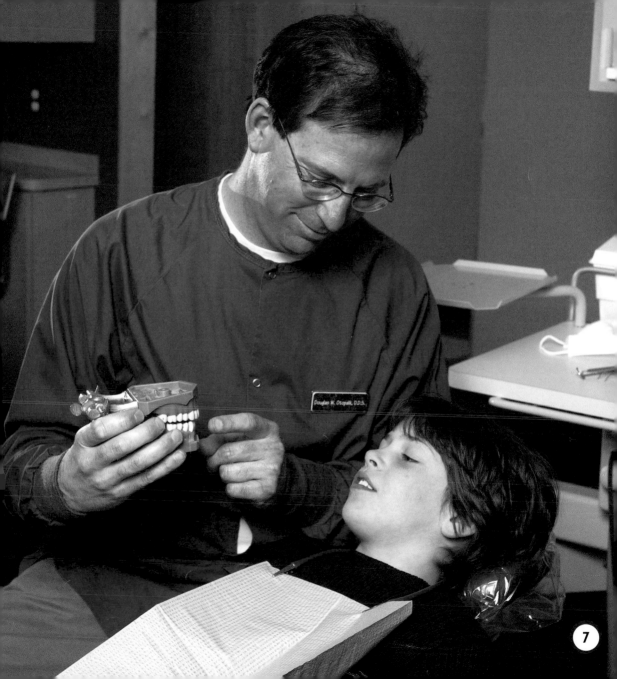

The dentist uses
special tools. He
shines a bright light
in your mouth.

- - - - - - - -

El dentista tiene
instrumentos especiales.
Usa una luz brillante
para mirarte en la boca.

The dentist looks at your teeth with a **mirror**. She checks your teeth with a tool called an **explorer**.

- - - - - - -

La dentista te mira los dientes con un **espejo**. Para examinarlos, usa un instrumento llamado **explorador**.

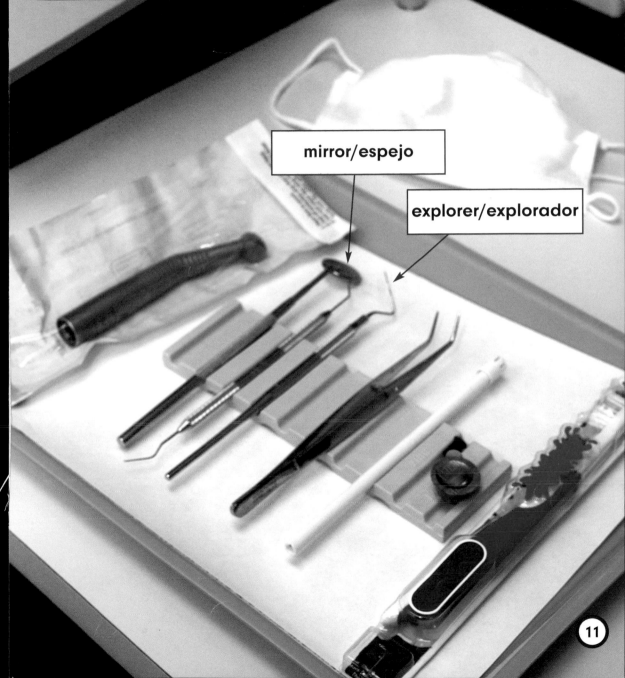

mirror/espejo

explorer/explorador

11

The dentist cleans your teeth. She shows you how to brush your teeth with a **toothbrush**.

- - - - - - -

La dentista te limpia la dentadura. Te enseña cómo cepillarte los dientes con un **cepillo**.

**toothbrush/
cepillo de dientes**

Sometimes the dentist takes **X-ray pictures** of your teeth with an X-ray machine.

– – – – – – – –

Algunas veces, el dentista te saca **fotografías de rayos-X** de la dentadura con una máquina de rayos-X.

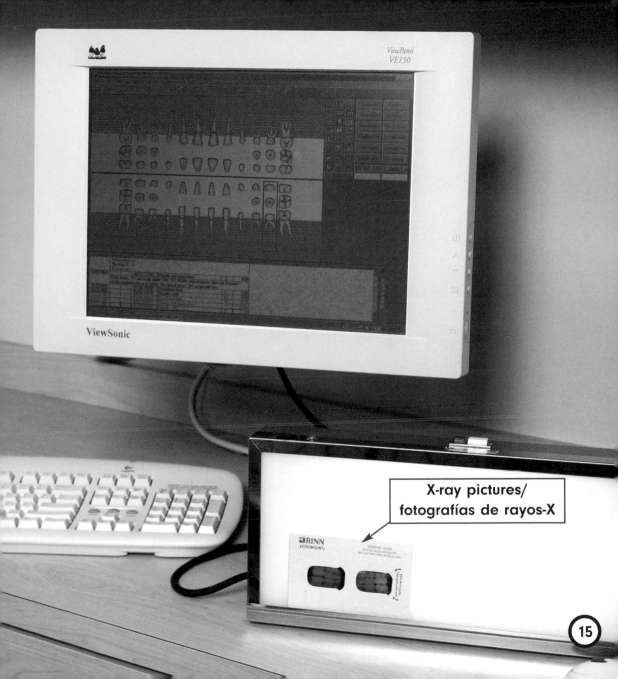

X-ray pictures/
fotografías de rayos-X

15

The dentist makes
you feel better if you
have a toothache.

- - - - - - - -

El dentista hace que
te sientas mejor
cuando tienes un
dolor de muelas.

You should visit the dentist two times a year. This keeps your teeth healthy.

- - - - - - - -

Debes ir a la dentista dos veces al año. Así tu dentadura se mantendrá sana.

It looks like fun to
be a dentist. Would
you like to be a dentist
some day?

— — — — — — —

Ser dentista parece
divertido. ¿Te gustaría
ser dentista algún día?

Glossary/Glosario

dentist — a doctor who takes care of your teeth
dentista — doctor que te cuida los dientes

explorer — a tool that dentists use to check and clean teeth
explorador — instrumento que usa el dentista para revisar los dientes y limpiarlos

mirror — a surface that reflects something
espejo — objeto en el que se reflejan las cosas

toothache — a pain in a tooth
dolor de muelas — dolor en los dientes

toothbrush — a tool that you use to clean your teeth
cepillo de dientes — instrumento para limpiar los dientes

For More Information/Más información

Fiction Books/Libros de ficción

Berenstain, Stan and Jan. *The Berenstain Bears Visit the Dentist.* New York: Random House, 1981.

Brown, Marc. *Arthur Tricks the Tooth Fairy.* New York: Random House, 1997.

Nonfiction Books/Libros de no ficción

Ready, Dee. *Dentists.* Mankato, Minn.: Bridgestone Books, 1998.

Schaefer, Lola M. *We Need Dentists.* Mankato, Minn.: Pebble Books, 2000.

Web Sites/Páginas Web

ADA Kids' Corner

www.ada.org/public/topics/kids/index.html

Games, information, and answers to questions about dental health

Going to the Dentist

www.kidshealth.org/kid/feel_better/people/go_dentist.html

What happens at the dentist's office

Index/Índice

About the Author/Información sobre la autora

Jacqueline Laks Gorman is a writer and editor. She grew up in New York City and began her career working on encyclopedias and other reference books. Since then, she has worked on many different kinds of books. She lives with her husband and children, Colin and Caitlin, in DeKalb, Illinois.

Jacqueline Laks Gorman es escritora y editora. Creció en Nueva York, y se inició en su profesión editando enciclopedias y otros libros de consulta. Desde entonces ha trabajado en muchos tipos de libros. Vive con su esposo y sus hijos, Colin y Caitlin, en DeKalb, Illinois.